# Eco Alert!

# WASTE AND RECYCLING

Rebecca Hunter

## SEA-TO-SEA
*Mankato Collingwood London*

This edition first published in 2012 by

Sea-to-Sea Publications
Distributed by Black Rabbit Books
P.O. Box 3263, Mankato, Minnesota 56002

9 8 7 6 5 4 3 2

Published by arrangement with the Watts
Publishing Group Ltd, London.

Library of Congress Cataloging-in-Publication Data

Hunter, Rebecca, 1935-
 Waste and recycling / by Rebecca Hunter.
     p. cm. -- (Eco alert)
 Includes index.
 ISBN 978-1-59771-299-6 (library binding)
 1.  Recycling (Waste)--Juvenile literature.  I. Title.
 TD794.5.W348 2012
 363.72'82--dc22

                          2011001203

Planning and production by
Discovery Books Limited
Managing Editor: Rachel Tisdale
Editor: Rebecca Hunter
Designer: Blink Media
Picture research: Tom Humphrey
Illustrations: Stefan Chabluk

February 2011
RD/6000006415/001

Photographs: **British Glass Manufacturers
Confederation:** page 11; **British Sugar:** page 26
both; **Corbis:** page 8 bottom (Jerry Arcieri), page 8
top (Thinkstock), page 10 (James L Amos),
page 22 (Heiko Wolfraum/dpa), page 29 (William
Manning); **Discovery Photo Library:** page 19 top
(Chris Fairclough); **Getty Images:** page 4, page 7
top (Christopher Furlong), page 13 (Justin
Sullivan), page 14 (Arthur Tilley), page 21 (Gregg
Brown); **Istock:** page 7 bottom (Mike Clarke),
page 23 (Miguel Malo); **NASA:** page 27; **Rebecca
Hunter:** page 15, page 19 bottom; **Shutterstock:**
Cover (SergioZ), page 5, page 9 (Agphotographer),
page 12 (Paul Prescott), page 17 (prism 68), page
18 (Shutterlist), page 24 (Kevin Fleming), page 28
(Monkey Business Images); **Wikimedia:** page 16,
(United States Navy, Photographer's Mate 2nd
Class, George Trian).

Every attempt has been made to clear copyright.
Should there be any inadvertent omission please
apply to the publisher for rectification.

# Contents

# A Wasteful World

Imagine what would happen if nobody took your garbage away. What would it be like if day after day, week after week, your trash piled up in your house and front yard?

Pretty soon you would be wading through plastic bottles and paper bags and rotting food. It would look terrible and the smell would be worse. If we don't control the amount of waste we throw away, this situation might actually happen!

We live in a very wasteful world. Almost everything we do creates waste. Everything we buy, everything we eat, and everything we use all produces waste that has to be disposed of in some way.

As the population of the world grows, the amount of garbage produced increases, too. The problem is not just that our society produces more waste today than ever before, but it is also doing it at a greater rate. Today we produce three times as much waste as we did in the 1960s.

⊙ A strike by garbage removal workers in Leeds, England, in October 2009 shows what city streets look like after just a few weeks when refuse piles up.

The large volumes of garbage we make creates not just a disposal problem, but is also a huge waste of **natural resources**. Unless things can be reused or **recycled**, everything we throw away has to be produced again out of new materials. More trees have to be cut down to make paper; more oil has to be refined to make plastic. Prevention of waste is a better solution than even the best way of disposing of it.

Disposal of garbage has become critical throughout the world. Where does the garbage come from? How do we get rid of it? How can we reduce the amount of it? Finding ways to deal with the garbage we produce is one of the major problems facing the world today.

⊘ A large proportion of our garbage is disposed of in **landfill** sites. But landfill is an ugly, polluting, and environmentally unfriendly way to dispose of waste.

# Domestic Waste

Many people buy a daily newspaper, drink cola from an aluminum can, or coffee from a polystyrene cup. All these things are used once and then thrown away.

## Inside the Trash Can

If we look at the waste an average household produces, you will see that the largest amount comes from leftover food and garden waste. After this, paper and cardboard are the biggest contributors. More than half of this comes from newspapers and magazines. Much of our garbage is plastic (packaging and bottles) and glass (bottles and jars), which makes up nearly one-quarter of our waste.

⊙ This piechart shows the proportions of the types of garbage produced in an average household.

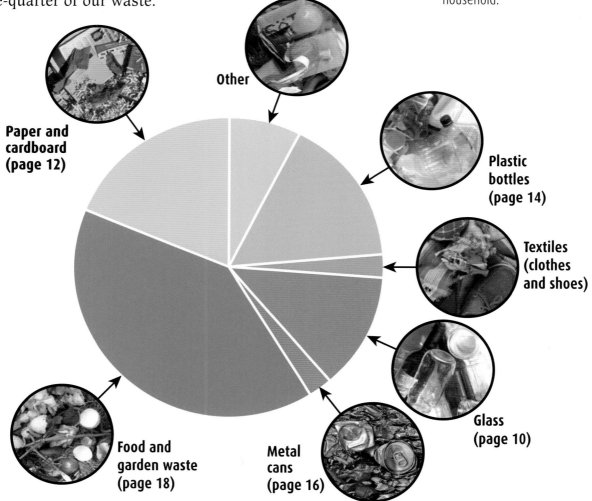

Other

Paper and cardboard (page 12)

Plastic bottles (page 14)

Textiles (clothes and shoes)

Glass (page 10)

Food and garden waste (page 18)

Metal cans (page 16)

## So Where Does It All Go?

Most people put their garbage into plastic bags and place the bag in a trash can. Then it is picked up by a garbage truck. Some waste products such as paper, glass, plastic, metal, and garden waste can be recycled and these are collected separately.

In most countries, the majority of waste that cannot be recycled is sent to landfill. This means it is buried in the ground. Some is **incinerated**, which means it is burned. Dealing with our garbage in this way is not a very good solution. When we bury or burn waste we are polluting the land and **atmosphere**. Most landfill sites are nearly full and we are running out of land for new sites.

⬤ The U.S. is the world's top garbage-producing country. On average, each person produces 1,610 pounds (730 kg) of garbage every year. This means a family of four will produce more than 3 tons of garbage a year.

Every nation needs to find ways of reducing the amount of waste they produce, recycling more of it, and disposing of what is left over more carefully.

▶ In most residential areas, household waste is picked up and taken away by garbage collectors. Most of it is disposed of in landfill sites or incinerated.

# Reduce, Reuse, Recycle

To help solve the waste problem we need to *reduce* the amount of garbage we create, *reuse* as much of our waste as possible, and *recycle* more of it.

## The Three Rs

There are three main reasons to reduce, reuse, and recycle.

- It saves natural resources. For example, if we reduce the amount of paper we use, we will cut down fewer trees.
- It stops pollution and reduces landfill.
- It saves money. Recycling is usually cheaper than making new things because it uses fewer resources and less energy.

### How can you help?

**REDUCE:** Most countries have a mailing preference service, which will remove your name and address from mailing lists, reducing the amount of junk mail you receive (right).

**REUSE:** Give old books and toys to playgroups, hospitals, or thrift stores.

**RECYCLE:** Turn food waste from your kitchen into compost for your garden.

⊛ Many products we buy are wrapped in unnecessary layers of packaging. If manufacturers used less packaging it would reduce the amount of waste in our trash cans by a huge amount.

# Waste Disposal by Country

How countries dispose of their waste often depends on their size. Large countries have a lot of space to bury their waste so Canada and the United States dispose of more than half their garbage in this way. Small countries do not have large areas of land available for landfill and so incinerate or recycle more of their garbage. For example, Japan and Denmark send more than half their garbage for incineration while Switzerland recycles a massive 76 percent of its garbage.

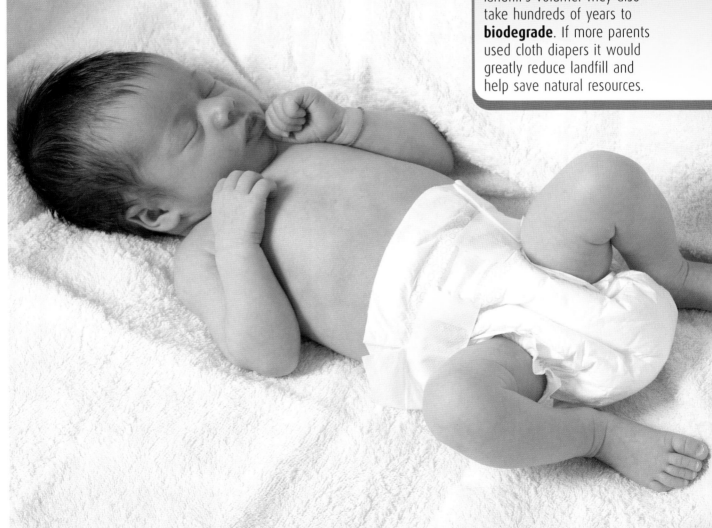

# Recycling Glass

Glass is a material that is particularly suitable for recycling. It can be melted down and used over and over again, without losing its quality or strength.

## The Recycling Process

You can take your waste glass to collection points, or some cities offer a curbside collection service. The glass is taken to a recycling plant where it is sorted into different colors, cleaned, and crushed. The crushed glass is called cullet and this is melted down and used in the production of new bottles or jars.

Piles of crushed glass at a recycling plant. Even if only half of the raw material used to make new glass is recycled, it reduces the waste involved in making new glass by 80 percent.

## Environmentally Friendly

Materials such as sand, limestone, and soda are used when making new glass, so recycling glass allows natural resources to be conserved. Energy can also be saved—resulting in a reduction in pollution, too. When new glass is made, the **furnace** has to be heated to a very high temperature, using huge amounts of energy. But when glass is recycled, the temperature of the furnace can be cooler, saving energy and reducing pollution.

These bottles are being made of recycled glass. The energy saved from recycling one glass bottle can run a 100-watt lightbulb for 4 hours.

## Big Business

In many countries, glass recycling has become a large and profitable business. In the United States glass recycling employs more than 30,000 workers in 76 factories. A typical American glass-processing factory can recycle up to 20 tons of glass per hour and nearly 13 million glass jars and bottles are recycled every day. It is thought that about 37 percent of the U.S.'s glass bottles and jars are now recycled, but the amount of glass recycled varies widely between different states.

### How can you help?

As well as recycling glass bottles and jars, think of other ways to use them. Fill them with homemade jam or jelly or decorate them and use them as flower vases or pencil holders.

# Recycling Paper

Disposing of paper is a big problem because we use such large amounts of it. Every day we read from it, write on it, and buy products wrapped in it. Most of this is thrown away after one use. An average household throws away 13,000 separate pieces of paper each year, made up mostly of packaging and junk mail.

### How can you help?

As well as recycling paper, try to reduce the amount you use and reuse more. Use both sides of a piece of paper, reuse wrapping paper, cut up old greeting cards to make new ones or use them as gift tags.

## Paper Problems

Paper production accounts for about 35 percent of all trees that are cut down and is responsible for more than 40 percent of landfill waste. Paper is biodegradable. An unfortunate side-effect of this is that it produces methane, a **greenhouse gas**, as it **decomposes**. This may contribute to **global warming**. If more waste paper was recycled, it would save trees and help protect the atmosphere.

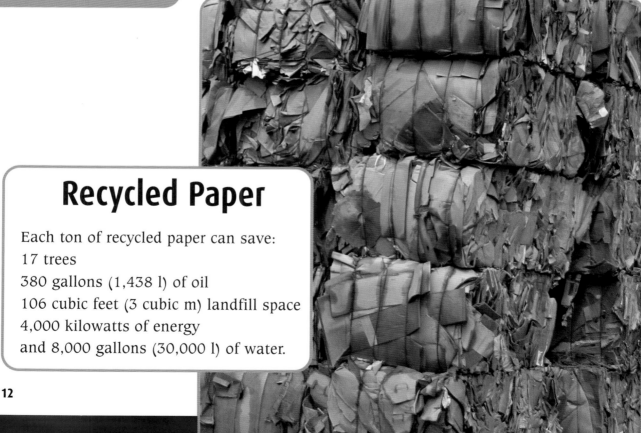

## Recycled Paper

Each ton of recycled paper can save:
17 trees
380 gallons (1,438 l) of oil
106 cubic feet (3 cubic m) landfill space
4,000 kilowatts of energy
and 8,000 gallons (30,000 l) of water.

## Processing Waste Paper

You can take your waste paper to collection points, or it may be picked up at the curb. It is taken to a paper mill where it is sorted, graded, and mixed with water to form a pulp. The pulp is cleaned and then made into new paper products. Producing recycled paper uses much less energy and water than making new paper from wood. Every ton of recycled paper can save enough electricity to run a three-bedroom house for one year.

This table shows the products recycled paper can be made into. What it is used for depends on the quality of the recycled paper.

| Quality | Use |
|---------|-----|
| High | Writing paper |
| Medium | Newspaper, wrapping paper, toilet paper |
| Low | Cardboard, packaging |

⊙ In California, the law requires that 50 percent of the paper used in producing newspapers should be recycled paper.

# Plastic

Today we use 20 times more plastic than we did 50 years ago. This increase means we have even more to get rid of, and disposing of it is not easy.

## The Problem with Plastic

At present, eight out of ten plastic bottles go into landfill. Plastic doesn't rot away. A plastic bottle could take 1,000 years before it even begins to decompose! However, if plastic is burned in an incinerator it emits **poisonous** gases that can pollute the atmosphere. Another problem with plastic is that it is made from oil, a natural resource that is running out. The best solution for getting rid of plastic is to recycle it. That way, we can stop wasting a precious natural resource and help the environment.

⊙ These children are visiting a **materials recovery facility** to see how plastic is recycled.

## Recycling Plastic

One of the problems with recycling plastic is that it is expensive to collect because it takes up a lot of space. That is why when you put your plastic bottles into recycling containers, you should squash the air out of them. At the recycling center, plastics are sorted into different types and colors before being shredded into chips and washed. The plastic chips are sent to a plastics factory where they are melted down and used to make new items. Did you know that clothing, and even baseball caps, can be made from recycled plastic bottles?

## Reducing Packaging

Many food products are wrapped in several layers of unnecessary plastic packaging, which is not recyclable. Manufacturers, retailers, and members of the public need to work together to reduce this wasteful use of plastic. In some countries, "green" campaigners are calling for all food packaging to be made recyclable by 2013.

### How can you help?

The best solution for the plastic problem is to try not to use it at all. Always take reusable bags with you instead of plastic ones when you go for groceries or if you are going out shopping to make other kinds of purchases.

⊽ Recycled plastic can be made into many unusual things. This floating boat jetty is composed of tough, interlocking blocks made of recycled plastic.

# Metals

Metals are widely used throughout the world to make items ranging from space rockets to beverage cans. They are found underground as **mineral ores**. These natural resources are limited, so we should conserve them by recycling as much metal as possible.

## Recycling Metals

The metals that are most easily recycled are aluminum and steel. We use them in many forms of food packaging, from beverage cans to yogurt carton caps. Before it can be recycled, metal is sorted into steel and aluminum at a waste-processing factory. The metals are then sent to a **smelting** works where they are melted down at a very high temperature. Recycled metal products include paper clips, scissors, office furniture, ladders, food and beverage cans, nails, and screws.

⊙ In one year in the U.S., the recycling of steel saves enough energy to heat and light 18 million homes!

# Useful Aluminum

Aluminum is one of the most successfully recycled substances. This is lucky because we use more than 80 billion aluminum beverage cans every year! Recycling aluminum saves 95 percent of the energy needed to produce new aluminum from **raw materials**, and there is no limit to the amount of times aluminum can be recycled. The energy saved from recycling one ton of aluminum is equal to the amount of electricity the average home uses over a period of ten years.

## How can you help?

Reuse metal coat hangers by taking them to your local dry cleaners. Many dry cleaners are trying to keep costs down by reusing coat hangers rather than buying new ones.

It is not possible to reuse beverage cans, so it is important to recycle them.

# Biodegradable Waste

About one-third of waste from households is biodegradable—that means it is capable of rotting away naturally. Biodegradable waste can include grass clippings, fruit and vegetable peelings, and other food waste. It also includes both human and animal waste. Biodegradable waste is also produced in large quantities by restaurants, businesses, and factories.

## Landfill Problems

You might think that waste that rots away would be suitable to dispose of in the ground as landfill. But actually this is not a good method of disposal. When biodegradable materials break down they produce methane, a greenhouse gas. For

⊙ We waste a shocking amount of food each year. On average, each year, every American throws away 1,200 pounds (544 kg) of biodegradable food waste, which could easily have been composted.

example, about one-quarter of the UK's methane emissions comes from landfill sites. This is about 2 percent of the UK's total greenhouse gas emissions. To reduce this amount, biodegradable waste needs to be reused and recycled.

## Recycling Options

On a small scale, biodegradable waste can be collected in a **compost** container. The waste is broken down by bacteria (tiny organisms) and eventually forms compost that can be used like **fertilizer** in the garden. However, many people live in towns or cities and don't have gardens to collect compost in. In some urban areas, waste is now collected from households and taken to a facility that has a **biodigester**. The biodigester processes the waste and captures the methane that is given off. This can be used for heating or cooking or to generate electricity. The solid waste that is left over is made into fertilizers.

### HOT SPOT:

#### Ludlow Biodigester

The people of Ludlow, in England, put their food waste in blue containers (above). Each week the food waste is collected from the containers and taken to a nearby biodigester where it is turned into compost, liquid fertilizer, and methane. More than 700 tons of food waste is recycled in this way each year.

◀ Small communities in **developing countries** often run their own biodigesters on animal manure. These men are making "logs" from the solid matter left over from their biodigester, which can be used as fuel for cooking and heating.

# Landfill and Incineration

So what happens to waste that cannot be reused or recycled? It either ends up in landfill or is burned in an incinerator. Neither of these options is ideal, but there will always be some garbage that cannot be disposed of in any other way. It is important therefore that both methods are carried out in a way that is least harmful to the environment.

## Landfill Design

Dumping millions of tons of garbage needs a lot of space. This has often been found in old quarries or mining works. In the past, landfills have created many environmental problems. Rats and pests, seeping liquid pollution, greenhouse gases, and litter blowing around are all unwanted side effects of landfill. Now however, landfills are designed much more carefully and are managed much better. Once landfill areas are full, they can be covered up and relandscaped to make parks or other types of recreational area.

▶ This diagram shows how a modern landfill site is constructed and managed.

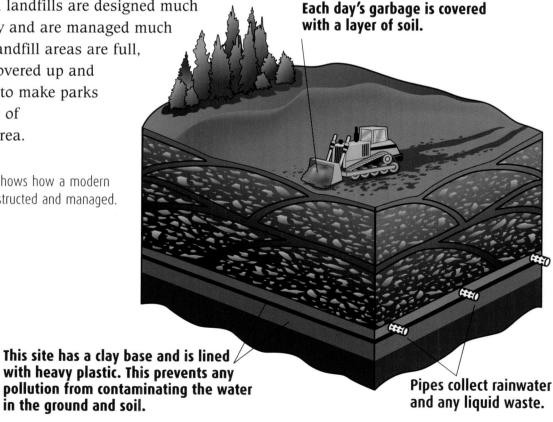

**Each day's garbage is covered with a layer of soil.**

**This site has a clay base and is lined with heavy plastic. This prevents any pollution from contaminating the water in the ground and soil.**

**Pipes collect rainwater and any liquid waste.**

The Fresh Kills landfill site in New York City is so large it can be seen from outer space! Covering 3.5 square miles (8.9 square km), it will shortly be closed and there are plans to develop the area into parklands.

## Incineration

Incineration is common in countries like Japan where land is more scarce. About three-quarters of Japan's waste is burned in incinerators. This burning of waste is used to recover energy (in the form of steam) for heating and for generating electricity, but it also emits a high concentration of polluting gases, which must be treated before being released into the atmosphere.

## Construction Industry Waste

One of the largest producers of waste is the construction industry. Much of this is packaging. Construction companies are now working with manufacturers to reduce the amount of packaging used. The construction industry aims to reduce material waste going to landfill by the year 2012 by 50 percent.

**HOT SPOT:**

**Too Much Packaging!**

Figures show that in a year, one company supplied 28 miles (46 km) of kitchen worktop, wrapped in 56 miles (90 km) of packaging! The company intends to train staff to handle products more carefully so they can reduce the amount of packaging they use.

# Dangerous Waste

**M**ost of our garbage may be ugly to look at and can take up a lot of space, but it is not actually dangerous. Some types of waste, however, are unsafe and more difficult to dispose of.

## Electrical Items

Every year people buy new televisions, computers, or cell phones. We change batteries and light bulbs without thinking about what they are made of. Many contain poisonous chemicals such as mercury or cadmium or polluting gases. These items need to be taken to specialized centers where they can be dismantled and the **hazardous** substances removed and disposed of properly.

### How can you help?

Recycle your cell phone. Some companies will pay for your old phone. More than 90 percent of the materials in cell phones can be recycled and used to make new products.

⊙ Cell phones contain cadmium, a poisonous metal. They are a hazard if discarded, but can be successfully recycled. Only 10 percent of cell phones are recycled in the United States each year.

## Hospital Waste

Hospitals generate many types of contaminated waste. Bed linen needs to be cleaned and dressings disposed of properly. Waste that is not properly treated can cause infections and dangerous diseases to spread.

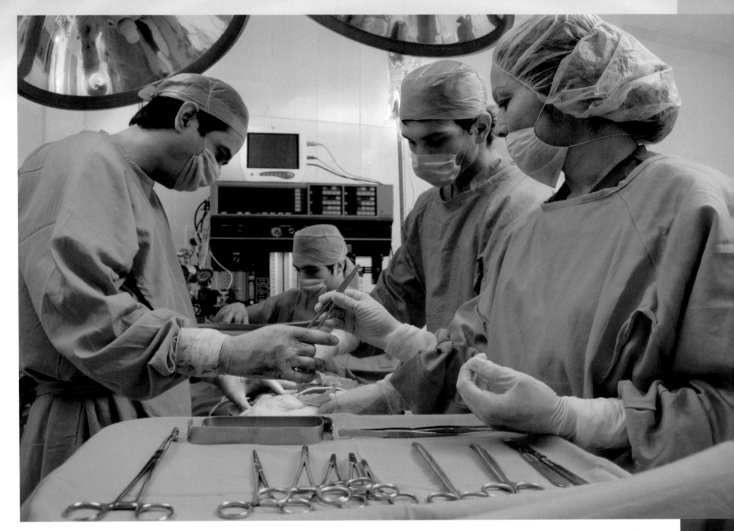

## Nuclear Waste

Nuclear power stations use **radioactive** materials to generate electricity. This process produces highly dangerous radioactive waste that will be buried in strong chambers deep underground for thousands of years. Although this waste is well contained, many people worry about the possibility of leakage if these areas were struck by earthquakes.

⊙ Surgical instruments can be sterilized at high temperatures and then used again, but needles, scalpels, and syringes must be incinerated.

23

# Industrial Waste

As well as the garbage we produce in our own households, a whole lot more is created by companies that manufacture products. Factories, mills, and mines all create waste and each type of industry has its own waste disposal problems.

## Thermal Pollution

Many industries, especially power plants, use water as a **coolant**. The water is used and returned to rivers, lakes, or sea at a higher temperature. This affects the **ecosystem** and fish and other animals can be killed by this "thermal shock." However, most industries try to prevent this by installing cooling towers or ponds, which transfer the heat to the atmosphere through **evaporation**.

⊙ Fish and other wildlife are at risk from polluted waterways.

## Water Pollution

The paper manufacturing industry uses more water per ton of product than any other industry. Vast quantities of water and chemicals are used to bleach the pulp, and then the water needs to be treated and cleaned after use.

⊕ The pulp and paper industry is the third-largest industrial polluter of air, water, and land in both Canada and the U.S., and releases well over 110,000 tons of toxic pollution each year. This paper mill in Brunswick, Georgia, sits on the Turtle River.

# Mining

Mining for coal, metal ores, and other precious metals or stones can damage the environment in several ways. Coal mining can leave huge holes in the ground and piles of unsightly **slag** that ruin the appearance of the landscape.

Gold mining is one of the dirtiest industries in the world. The production of just one gold ring generates 20 tons of mining waste. Open-pit gold mining uses a method where piles of crushed rock are soaked in a dangerous **cyanide** solution to extract the gold. If this solution is not carefully contained, it can pollute the surrounding soil and water, killing many plants and animals and sometimes local people.

**HOT SPOT:**

**Saying "No" to Dirty Gold**

Fourteen leading jewelry retailers from the UK and U.S. have said they will not buy gold from a proposed open-pit gold mine in Alaska. The proposed site is in an area of pristine wilderness, famous for its wild salmon.

# Waste Gases

Many industries and factories produce unwanted waste gases. A lot of these are poisonous or damaging to the environment.

## Carbon Dioxide

Burning **fossil fuels**, such as coal, oil, and gas, releases carbon dioxide ($CO_2$) into the atmosphere. The level of this greenhouse gas has risen over the last 30 years and is thought to be responsible for the global warming of the world. Despite this, fossil fuels continue to be burned at an increasing rate because it is the cheapest way of producing electricity. Many countries have plans to reduce the amount of $CO_2$ they release by storing it underground using a method called **carbon capture and storage**. However, this process has not yet been fully tested, and nobody knows if it will work.

### HOT SPOT:

### Greenhouse Gases in Greenhouses!

Sometimes $CO_2$ can be recycled. At this sugar beet factory in the UK (below), waste $CO_2$ from the sugar production process is piped into nearby greenhouses to increase the **yield** of fruits and vegetables grown there.

# Chlorofluorocarbons

Refrigerators used to contain chemicals called chlorofluorocarbons (CFCs). When an old refrigerator was scrapped, the CFCs were released into the atmosphere. These were found to be destroying the **ozone layer**. This layer of gas in the upper atmosphere is very important because it filters out **ultraviolet radiation** from the Sun. Most countries banned the use of CFCs in the 1990s and old refrigerators must now be taken to special recycling centers to be dismantled. The ozone hole is now shrinking, though full recovery may not happen until about 2070.

This image shows the ozone hole (shown in pink) over Antarctica.

# Methane

Methane is another greenhouse gas. It is thought that 18 percent of the **greenhouse effect** is caused by methane. It is produced by living things in a variety of ways; by rice paddy fields; by swamps and wetlands; by grazing animals; and, as we have seen, from rotting waste in landfill. We cannot do much about most of these sources, but the methane produced in landfill can be captured and used to generate electricity. The United States is currently spending $400 million building facilities at 60 landfills throughout the country to do this.

## How can you help?

Help save the atmosphere by reducing the amount of electricity you use. Turn off lights and other electrical appliances when not in use.

# A Low-Waste Future

The United Nations estimates worldwide annual waste production to be at more than two billion tons, and increasing every year. It is clear that we need to impose stricter regulations on the creation and disposal of our waste.

## Preventing Waste

The way we deal with waste can be shown in a pyramid diagram. Now, most of our waste goes to landfill or is burned. This is the worst option. Further up the pyramid we reduce, reuse, and recycle waste. The prevention of waste—the best option—is the least common, at the top. What we need to do is reverse the pyramid so that the largest volume of waste is prevented from occurring, and landfill and incineration options are greatly reduced.

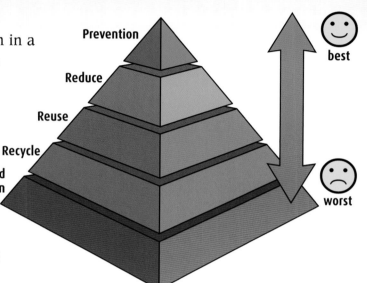

Prevention

Reduce

Reuse

Recycle

Landfill and incineration

best

worst

## HOT SPOT:

### Chinese Chopsticks

The Chinese use 45 billion pairs of disposable chopsticks a year, using the wood from 25 million trees. The Chinese government has now put a tax on disposable chopsticks and has urged restaurants not to use them. As a result, more than 400 restaurants in Beijing have promised to wash and reuse their chopsticks!

## Dispose of Disposables

There are many ways in which you can help prevent making waste. Have you noticed how many disposable products are available today? Disposable cameras, disposable razors, disposable diapers, disposable cups, plates, and cutlery, batteries, and, of course, plastic bags. Try to buy reusable things rather than disposable ones.

## Working Together to Make Less

Much work needs to be done by governments and manufacturing industries to reduce the volume of waste created by the world. But every one of us can take part in controlling our waste. Every battery you don't buy, every bag you reuse, and every bottle you recycle is helping reduce the pressure of waste on our planet.

New York City spends around $1 million a day on moving garbage. Here a tugboat pushes a barge filled with crushed cars.

# Glossary

**Atmosphere**
The layer of gases that surrounds the Earth.

**Biodegradable**
Something that will break down and rot naturally.

**Biodigester**
A machine that can process plant and animal waste to create electricity.

**Carbon capture and storage**
A method of storing carbon dioxide produced from power plants.

**Compost**
Decayed plant material that can be used to improve soil.

**Coolant**
A liquid, usually water, used to prevent overheating.

**Cyanide**
A very poisonous chemical.

**Decompose**
To break down through the action of bacteria and fungi.

**Developing countries**
Poorer countries where people have a low standard of living and low levels of industry.

**Ecosystem**
A community of living things together with their environment.

**Evaporation**
When something changes from a liquid into a gas.

**Fertilizer**
Chemicals that are put on the land to help the growth of crops.

**Fossil fuels**
Fuels such as coal, oil, and natural gas that were formed underground millions of years ago.

**Furnace**
A very hot oven used to melt metals.

**Global warming**
A rise in the average temperature of the Earth, which many people think is caused by an increase of greenhouse gases in the atmosphere.

**Greenhouse effect**
The warming of the Earth caused by a layer of insulating gases.

**Greenhouse gases**
Gases in the atmosphere, such as carbon dioxide or water vapor, that absorb heat that would otherwise escape into space.

**Hazardous**
Very dangerous.

**Incinerate**
To burn to ashes.

**Landfill**
A place where waste materials are buried in the ground.

**Materials recovery facility**
A place where waste materials are sorted.

**Mineral ores**
Rocks that contain metals.

**Natural resources**
Resources that are available naturally on the Earth, such as wood, oil, coal, and water.

**Ozone layer**
The layer of ozone gas in the atmosphere.

**Poisonous**
Containing dangerous substances.

**Radioactive**
Capable of giving out energy in the form of powerful and harmful rays.

**Raw materials**
The basic material from which a product is made.

**Recycle**
The act of processing used materials for use in making new products.

**Slag**
A mixture of coal dust and rock waste that is left over after coal has been mined.

**Smelting**
Melting a mineral ore to get metal from it.

**Ultraviolet radiation**
Invisible rays from the Sun that can damage the skin and cause skin cancer.

**Yield**
The amount of crop produced.

# Further Information

## Books

*Food and Garden Waste (What happens when we recycle?)*
Jillian Powell, Franklin Watts, 2009

*Refuse Collection (How It Works)*
James Nixon, Franklin Watts, 2009

*Waste and Pollution (Sustaining our Environment)*
Jill Laidlaw, Franklin Watts, 2009

*Waste and Recycling (The Green Team)*
Sally Hewitt, Franklin Watts, 2008

*Dealing with Waste* series
Sally Morgan, Franklin Watts, 2006

## Web Sites

**http://tonto.eia.doe.gov/kids/energy.cfm?page=environment_recycling-basics**
Learn all about recycling from the Energy Information Administration.

**www.ecy.wa.gov/programs/swfa/kidsPage**
An interactive site designed to illustrate the importance of waste reduction, recycling, and solid waste management.

**www.epa.gov/recyclecity/**
Welcome to Recycle City. Find out how the people of Dumptown learned to reduce waste, save money, and turn their town around.

**www.recycling-revolution.com/**
All you need to know about recycling, reducing waste, sustainable lifestyles, and even how to make cash from trash!

Note to parents and teachers: Every effort has been made by the publishers to ensure that these web sites are suitable for children and that they contain no inappropriate or offensive material. However, because of the nature of the Internet, it is impossible to guarantee that the contents of these sites will not be altered. We strongly advise that Internet access is supervised by a responsible adult.

# Index